Especially for

_____

From

_____

Date

_____

© 2013 by Barbour Publishing, Inc.

Print ISBN 978-1-62029-807-7

eBook Editions:
Adobe Digital Edition (.epub) 978-1-62416-018-9
Kindle and MobiPocket Edition (.prc) 978-1-62416-017-2

Devotional readings are taken from *Daily Wisdom for Mothers* by Michelle Medlock Adams, *God's Word for Mothers*, and *Daily Whispers of Wisdom for Single Mothers*, all published by Barbour Publishing, Inc.

Scripture quotations marked KJV are taken from the King James Version of the Bible.

Scripture quotations marked NIV are taken from the HOLY BIBLE, NEW INTERNATIONAL VERSION®. NIV®. Copyright © 1973, 1978, 1984, 2011 by Biblica, Inc.™ Used by permission. All rights reserved worldwide.

Scripture quotations marked NLT are taken from the *Holy Bible*. New Living Translation copyright© 1996, 2004, 2007 by Tyndale House Foundation. Used by permission of Tyndale House Publishers, Inc. Carol Stream, Illinois 60188. All rights reserved.

Scripture quotations marked CEV are from the Contemporary English Version, Copyright © 1995 by American Bible Society. Used by permission.

Scripture quotations marked NKJV are taken from the New King James Version®. Copyright © 1982 by Thomas Nelson, Inc. Used by permission. All rights reserved.

Published by Barbour Publishing, Inc., P.O. Box 719, Uhrichsville, Ohio 44683, www.barbourbooks.com

Our mission is to publish and distribute inspirational products offering exceptional value and biblical encouragement to the masses.

ecpa Member of the
Evangelical Christian
Publishers Association

Printed in China.

Wisdom for Mothers

Devotional Journal

BARBOUR
PUBLISHING

Moments of Peace

*"Come to me, all you who are weary
and burdened, and I will give you rest."*
MATTHEW 11:28 NIV

Ahhh. . .rest. Who wouldn't love a day of rest? But let's face it.
Mothers don't really get a day of rest. If we rested, who would fix
breakfast? Who would get the children ready for church? Who would
do the laundry so your son can wear his lucky socks for the big game
on Monday?

No, there's not a lot of rest in a mother's schedule. But, that's not
really the kind of rest this verse is talking about. The rest mentioned
in this verse is the kind of rest that only Jesus can provide. Resting in
Jesus means feeling secure in Him and allowing His peace to fill your
soul. That kind of rest is available to all—even mothers.

So, in the midst of the hustle and bustle of your life (even if you're
elbow deep in dishwater), you can rest in Him. Start by meditating on
the Lord's promises and His everlasting love for you. Make a mental
list of the things in your life that you are thankful for, and praise God
for each one. Allow His love to overwhelm you. . .and rest.

*Lord, help me to rest in You—
even when I'm overwhelmed with the "to-dos"
of each day. I want more of You in my life.
I love You. Amen.*

Just Trust Me!

*Trust in the LORD with all your heart;
do not depend on your own understanding.*

PROVERBS 3:5 NLT

How often we have told our children, "Don't run in the street"? Or, "Don't touch the stove"? Or, "Do your homework—your education is important"? Or, "Don't fool around with drugs"? Or how about this one: "Just trust me, will you?"

There will be times when we need our children to simply trust us. Times when they need to stop questioning, stop asking why, and simply obey—even when they don't understand the reasons. We tell them to trust that we know best.

In the same way, God wants us to obey Him—even though we may not understand and just can't figure out why. "Simply obey My word," He says. We may not fully "get it," yet He asks us to trust Him in spite of our lack of complete understanding.

We can always trust Him to know what's best. That's what we desire from our own children—and that's what our heavenly Father wants from us.

Father God, if we as sinful human beings show true concern for our children, how could we ever think You would do any less? Forgive me for trusting my own understanding rather than Your wisdom.

More Than a Woman

I can do everything through him who gives me strength.
PHILIPPIANS 4:13 NIV

Remember that powerful song "I Am Woman" performed by Helen Reddy? Sometimes it's empowering to belt out the lyrics: "I am strong. I am invincible. I am WOMAN!" Aren't those empowering words?

There are some days when we can't muster the courage to sing, "I am woman, hear me roar. . . ." In fact, we may feel more like singing, "I'm a worm on the floor." How about you? Do you ever feel less than powerful?

Well, there's news, and it's even better than Helen Reddy's song. God's Word says that we can do all things through Christ who gives us strength. All means all, right? So no matter how you feel today, you can accomplish whatever is on your plate. See, you don't have to feel powerful to be powerful. The God in you is all-powerful, and He will cause you to triumph. After all, you are more than a woman—you are a child of the Most High God. Now that's something to sing about!

*Thank You, Lord, that even when
I feel powerless, You are powerful.
Help me to be courageous for You. Amen.*

No Worries

*"Can any one of you by worrying add
a single hour to your life?"*
MATTHEW 6:27 NIV

If you're an '80s lady, you probably remember that catchy song "Don't Worry, Be Happy." (You're singing it right now, aren't you?) Truth be told, there's a lot of truth in that silly little song.

So many times, as mothers, we think it's our job to worry. After all, if we don't worry about the children, who will? Someone has to worry about their grades, their health, and their futures—right?

Well. . .not exactly. God tells us in His Word that worry is a profitless activity. Worrying about our children may feel like a natural thing to do as a mother, but in reality it's sin. Here's why. If we are constantly worrying about our kids, that means we're not trusting God to take care of them. It's like saying to God, "I know that You created the universe, but I'm not sure You know what's best for my children. So, I'll handle these kids, God."

When you put it that way, it sounds ridiculous, doesn't it? We would never say that to God, yet each time we give in to worry, that's the message we're communicating. So, do like the song says, "Don't Worry, Be Happy." God's got you covered!

*Father, I give all of my worries to You.
I trust You with my children. I love You. Amen.*

The Land of "What If"

*"For I know the plans I have for you," declares the L*ORD*, "plans to prosper you and not to harm you, plans to give you hope and a future."*
JEREMIAH 29:11 NIV

Do you ever feel like you're not doing enough for your children? Sure, you enrolled them in ballet, karate, and gymnastics, but you forgot to sign them up for soccer—and now it's too late! The recording in your head begins playing, "You're a bad mother."

We all hear that same recording. Sometimes, it plays nonstop.

We worry that we're not providing our children with the opportunities that will bring success. What if they don't make the middle school soccer team because I didn't sign them up for summer soccer camp? What if they miss out on those academic scholarships because I didn't spend enough time reading with them when they were little?

What if? What if? What if?

You know, God doesn't want us dwelling in the land of "What If." He wants us to trust Him with our children. He wants us to quit "what if-ing!" God has a plan for their lives—better than you could ever imagine. So, relax. You're not a bad mother because you missed soccer camp sign-ups. If you've given your children to God, you've given them the best chance to succeed that you could ever give them!

Lord, I give my children to You.
Thank You, God, for Your plans. Amen.

Miss America Mom

*"The Lord does not look at the things people look at.
People look at the outward appearance,
but the Lord looks at the heart."*

1 Samuel 16:7 niv

You know her: she's the mom who has a flat belly, long legs, and perfect hair. Admit it, you occasionally wish she'd fall into a cotton candy machine and gain thirty pounds. Her very presence makes you feel less than attractive, doesn't it?

Comparing ourselves with others is never a good thing, and it's not a God thing, either. God isn't concerned with whether or not your belly is as trim as it was before childbirth. His Word says that He looks on the heart, not on your outward appearance. He's more concerned with the condition of your heart, not the cellulite on your legs. Of course, that doesn't mean we shouldn't strive to be the best we can be—both inside and out—but it certainly relieves some of that pressure to be perfect.

Give your jealousies and feelings of inadequacy to God and find your identity in Him. He loves you just the way you are—even if you're not Miss America.

*Father, help me not to compare myself with others.
Help me to see myself through Your eyes. Amen.*

Rejoice

You shall rejoice in all the good things the LORD
your God has given to you and your household.
DEUTERONOMY 26:11 NIV

*R*ejoice in the Lord always. Again I will say, rejoice!" (Philippians 4:4 NKJV). That's what the Word says, but that's not always the easiest task, to say the least. What about when your child's teacher says something ugly about Junior during your parent/teacher conference? Or, how about when another driver pulls right in front of you and steals your parking spot at the grocery store? Or when your toddler knocks over your red fingernail polish, spilling it all over your bathroom rug? Not wanting to rejoice too much at that point, are you?

Daily aggravations will be a part of life until we get to heaven. That's a fact. So, we just have to learn how to deal with those aggravations.

Here's the plan: today if something goes wrong—stop, pause, and praise. You don't have to praise God for the aggravation. That would be kind of silly. Praise God *in spite* of the aggravation. Before long, the "stop, pause, and praise" practice will become a habit. And that's the kind of habit worth forming! So go on, start rejoicing!

Father, I repent for the times when I am less than thankful.
I rejoice in You today. Amen.

What's in Your Heart?

"The good man brings good things out of the good stored up in his heart, and the evil man brings evil things out of the evil stored up in his heart. For the mouth speaks what the heart is full of."
LUKE 6:45 NIV

Are you an angry person? In other words, do you have a short fuse? If you do, chances are your tongue betrays you all the time. Angry people typically retaliate with words—angry, hurtful words—at a moment's notice. They are quick to attack and slow to repent.

When we get angry, we often say things we don't mean. But, according to Luke 6:45, we actually speak what is in our hearts. That's a scary thought, isn't it? Who knew all of that yucky stuff was stored up in our hearts? Sometimes it's explained like this: If you squeeze a tube of toothpaste, toothpaste comes out. If you put pressure on a person who is full of ugliness and anger, ugly and angry words come out.

So, here's the key: we need to store up more of God in our hearts so that when the pressure is on, godly words will flow out of us. In other words, when our true colors are revealed, they will be the colors of Christ. Go ahead; fill up on God!

*Heavenly Father, I want more of You and less of me.
Please take away the angry part of me. Amen.*

A Lesson from Daniel

Now when Daniel learned that the decree had been published,
he went home to his upstairs room where the windows opened toward
Jerusalem. Three times a day he got down on his knees and prayed,
giving thanks to his God, just as he had done before.

DANIEL 6:10 NIV

Are you too busy to pray? Do you run 100 mph all day long? That's why we need to take a lesson from Daniel. Daniel was a wise man. He learned that in order to hear from God, he needed to slow down. As you can read here in the sixth chapter of Daniel, he stopped and dropped to his knees three times a day to pray to God. He knew that he needed to hear from God before continuing on. He knew that God was more than worth his time.

We should realize that same truth, too. No matter how busy we become with our motherly duties, we need to take time to pray. We need to seek His face on a regular basis. If we don't, we'll just be spinning our wheels. So, don't neglect your prayer time. Give time to God, and He will give time back to you. He isn't working against you, He is working *for* you. And together, the two of you can't lose!

Lord, help me to slow down in order to hear from You. Amen.

Teaching the Word

Since you have forgotten the laws of your God,
I will forget to bless your children.
HOSEA 4:6 NLT

❁

As moms, it's our awesome responsibility to tell our children about the things of God. If we don't tell them about salvation, they'll never know that Jesus died on the cross to save them from sin. If we don't tell them about His unconditional love, they won't run to Him in times of trouble. If we don't tell them about healing, they'll never know that God can heal their sicknesses. They need to know these important truths so that they won't perish for lack of knowledge.

Teaching our children God's Word and His ways are the two most important things we can give our kids, because if they have that knowledge, they have it all! As moms, we can't always be there for our children. But if we've equipped them with the Word of God, they will be all right without us.

It's like John Cougar Mellencamp says in one of his '80s tunes, "You've got to stand for something, or you're going to fall for anything." If our children stand on the Word of God, they won't be easily fooled or swayed. So, take the time to teach your children the Word. It's the most important investment you'll ever make.

❁

Heavenly Father, help my children to love
Your Word and carry it with them always. Amen.

Praise Him

Have you ever heard the expression, "Praise and be raised, or complain and remain"? Now that's a phrase that really packs a punch! It means if you complain about your current circumstances, you'll remain there a lot longer than if you'd just praise the Lord in spite of it all.

Sure that's easy to say, but it's not so easy to do. Praising God during difficult times is usually the last thing we want to do. We'd rather retreat to the bedroom with a box of Junior Mints and sulk awhile. But sulking won't change things any more than complaining will.

By praising God during the dark times, we're telling God that we trust Him—even though we can't see the daylight. Anyone can trust God and praise Him on the mountaintop, but only those who really know God's faithfulness can praise Him in the valley. And it's during those valley times that we truly feel God's tender mercy and experience extreme spiritual growth. So, praise God today—even if you don't feel like it. Through your praise, you open the door for God to work in your life.

Lord, I praise You in spite of the difficulties in my life.
Help me to resist complaining and praise You instead. Amen.

Reach Out and Touch

*She thought, "If I just touch
his clothes, I will be healed."*
MARK 5:28 NIV

*W*e should never underestimate the power of touch. In our busy
lives, as we rush from one appointment to another, skimping on
affection with our families and loved ones can become routine. We
wave good-bye to our children without stopping for a hug. Husbands
head off to work with the barest brush of a kiss.

We do our loved ones a disservice when we skip touching them.
Touching communicates our affection but also our affirmation and
sympathy. The Bible records Jesus touching many people, comforting
and healing them. He also let people touch Him, such as the sinful
woman who touched and kissed His feet (Luke 7:38).

In Mark 5, however, the true power of a simple touch is beautifully
portrayed. This woman who had suffered for so long believed so
strongly in Jesus that she knew the quickest touch of His hem would
heal her. She reached out, and her faith made her well.

So hold those you love close, and let them see a bit of Jesus' love in
you every day.

*Lord, I turn to You when I need comfort. Let me also
offer those around me the comfort of a loving touch. Amen.*

Bedtime Blessings

But when you pray, go into your room,
close the door and pray to your Father, who is unseen.
MATTHEW 6:6 NIV

Do you have a sort of bedtime ritual with your children? Some parents read a storybook to their children every night. Other parents share a Bible story or two. Some even make up their own stories to share. Whatever your bedtime routine might be, consider making prayer part of it.

Saying a bedtime prayer with your children is one of the most important things you can do for them. It accomplishes several things, such as teaching your kids to pray by hearing you pray aloud, giving prayer a place of importance in their lives, making prayer a habit for them, drawing the family unit closer, and enriching their spiritual side.

We spend so much time just doing "stuff" with our kids—running them to soccer practice, helping with homework, playing board games—and all of that is good. But if we don't figure prayer time into the daily equation, we're just spinning our wheels. Prayer time is a precious time. Don't miss out on it even one night. It's a habit worth forming!

Father, help me to teach my children
the importance of prayer time. Amen.

A Day of Rest

*Six days thou shalt do thy work, and on the seventh day thou
shalt rest: that thine ox and thine ass may rest, and the son
of thy handmaid, and the stranger, may be refreshed.*

EXODUS 23:12 KJV

If there is one scriptural principle that women routinely abandon,
it is that of the Sabbath. Because Christ has become our rest and
because we now worship on the Lord's Day, we often disregard the
idea of a Sabbath rest.

Rest was at the heart of the Sabbath. One day out of seven, God's
people were not to work or to make others work, so they could all be
refreshed.

God Himself started the work-rest pattern before the earth was a
week old. God didn't rest because He was tired; He rested because His
work of creation was finished.

But a woman's work is never done! How can she rest?

It's not easy. There are always more things that can be done. But
most of those things can wait a day while you recharge.

God's design for the week gives rest to the weary. Let's not neglect
His provision.

*Father, help me to rest from my labor as You
rested from Yours. Refresh me this day. Amen.*

A Laugh a Day

Shout praises to the LORD*, everyone on this earth.*
Be joyful and sing as you come in to worship the LORD*!*
PSALM 100:1–2 CEV

There's an old saying that "laughter is the best medicine." But it's actually more than that.

The Bible tells us that laughter is a *gift*. We should rejoice in the Lord and bring our gift of laughter to Him.

Sometimes, as a mom, you just have to laugh. Maybe you and your young son have just enjoyed a funny movie together. Or perhaps your teenage daughter thought it would be cool to dye her hair purple. In these cases, laughter can be both a song of praise and a catharsis.

It's important to find joy in the events of everyday life, and you should schedule time to pursue a good laugh after a tough week. Call some friends for a girls' night movie party or curl up with a funny book. Maybe you could listen to a Christian comedian for some good, clean humor and worship through laughter.

Whatever the source, make time to laugh—and send those giggles up to God.

Dear God, thank You for giving us the gift of laughter.
Help me to find joy in my daily life—and to make
time to laugh with family and friends.

He's Watching!

The eyes of the LORD are on the righteous,
and his ears are attentive to their cry.
PSALM 34:15 NIV

Does it seem strange to think that God is watching everything we do? As if He's a traffic cop, hiding behind a billboard, waiting to catch us doing something wrong?

Replace that mental image with the memory of the first time you held your baby in your arms. Or when you watched your child play at a playground. Or act in a school play. Or sing in the church choir. Your eyes scanned the crowd, searching for that familiar little face. You couldn't keep your eyes off your child. *That child belongs to me!* you thought.

God is watching each one of us with the same intense love with which we watch our children. His ability to be near us every moment is no threat—it's a promise. A guarantee! His Word tells us that He is near to everyone who calls out His name. We belong to Him! He can't keep His eyes off us.

Lord, why is it so hard to believe that You love me? Your Word reassures me, over and over, yet still, I doubt. Remind me again, Lord. Convince me! Draw close! Open my eyes to Your presence.

Starry Skies

Lift up your eyes and look to the heavens: Who created all these?
He who brings out the starry host one by one and calls forth
each of them by name. Because of his great power and
mighty strength, not one of them is missing.

ISAIAH 40:26 NIV

Everyone should spend some time stargazing. When we slow the frantic pace of our minds and look to the heavens, we begin to sense the unmatchable power, the sustaining strength, and the intimate love of God. As we gaze with admiration at the stars, we can drink in the very essence of our heavenly Creator.

It was God who hung every star in place. It's God who knows each star by name. Nothing in the farthest reaches of the universe goes unnoticed by God, because He's a God of order and intimacy.

If God cares that deeply about His starry creation, how much greater is His love for us, His cherished daughters?

Father, You are the Creator of all. I thank You that I can take in the awesome vastness of the universe and rest in peace—knowing not only that You are the master Creator, but that You hold me.

Support Staff

Our LORD, we belong to you. We tell you
what worries us, and you won't let us fall.
PSALM 55:22 CEV

Moms are the unsung heroes, the support staff, the ones everyone depends on. Our purses hold everything from bandages to granola bars to tissues. If you need it, we'll find it. But there are days when we tire of carrying the weight of the world. Sometimes we run ourselves ragged taking care of everyone—everyone, that is, except for ourselves.

There came a time when Elijah grew tired of caring for Israel. Worn out, he ran for the hills, contemplating early retirement. In fact, he hoped God would give him a break and end it all. "Just kill me," Elijah begged God. He was *that* exhausted.

Was God angry with Elijah for seeking an escape? Did God stand over Elijah, wagging a finger, telling him to pull it together?

Just the opposite! Tenderly, oh so tenderly, God sent angels to care for Elijah. They provided food and rest and encouragement.

Sometimes we're so busy and tired we have nothing left to give. During those times, remember Elijah. Rest, eat, nourish yourself. Just let God be in charge for a while.

Dear Lord, teach me to ask for help. Prod me to take better care of myself. Thank You for Your gentle response to my low periods. Remind me that things will get better again! They always do.

A Little Time with God

*"I thank You and praise You, O God of my fathers;
You have given me wisdom and might."*
DANIEL 2:23 NKJV

Susan headed out of her house in the same way she always did—in a hurry, double-checking her children's backpacks as she went and reminding them of chores and practices scheduled for that afternoon. "Remember, 3:30 is ballet; 4:00 is soccer. I'll pick you up after school, but I have to go back to work, so—"

She stopped as her coat snagged on a bush. As she stooped to untangle the cloth, the stem bent suddenly, and Susan found herself nose-to-petal with a rose. It smelled glorious, and she paused, laughing.

Susan glanced up toward the sky. "Thanks for grabbing me. I guess I should spend a little more time with You."

God blesses us every day in both great and simple ways. Children, friends, work, faith—all these things form a bountiful buffet of gifts, and caring for them isn't always enough. We need to spend a little time with the One who has granted us the blessings.

*Father God, You have given us so much to be grateful for.
Show me a way to spend more time with You,
and help me to grow closer and know You better. Amen.*

Treading Water

Then he went up on a mountain where he could be alone and pray.
Later that evening, he was still there.

MATTHEW 14:23 CEV

Treading water is not a sign of weakness. It's a tactic swimmers employ before their strength begins to fail. When weariness comes on, the swimmer stops pulling herself through the water, instead gently moving her arms and legs ever so slightly to remain above water. No progress is made while treading water, but time is gained for strength to recover.

Moms often feel like they're drowning—losing strength as the waters overtake them. So "treading water" for a time may be the best choice. We won't make any great advancements during that time—but a conscious decision to take no large steps, address no big issues, and simply rest can be exactly what we need to regroup.

Tread water for a few days, even weeks, if necessary. Reconnect with God through prayer and introspection. Let the Holy Spirit renew your soul and body so you can begin the journey once again with a new vigor.

Jesus, please renew and reenergize me as a parent
and as a believer. Through rest and prayer, please
strengthen me and return me to the vigor I once felt. Amen.

As Close as a Prayer

How long wilt thou forget me, O LORD? for ever?
how long wilt thou hide thy face from me?
PSALM 13:1 KJV

There is no worse feeling than feeling a distance from God. When we cry out in prayer, we need to feel His presence with us. When that feeling is absent, hopelessness and despair set in. We need to know, however, that the Lord has not really gone far from us, but we have pushed Him from ourselves. The Lord is always as close as a prayer, and we need to open our hearts to Him, and His presence will be felt once again. The Lord never hides His face from us, though often He will wait, stepping back like the loving Father He is, to see whether or not we can struggle through a problem on our own. God wants to see us grow, and He often has to let us struggle a bit in order to allow that growth to occur. Even in those times of trial, however, the Lord is never far away, and He will not allow us to be tried beyond our endurance.

Help me to know that You are with me in every situation at every moment of the day. I need Your comforting presence in my life, O Lord. Without it, I cannot go on. Amen.

The Father Has Bestowed a Great Love

Think how much the Father loves us. He loves us so much that he lets us be called his children, as we truly are. But since the people of this world did not know who Christ is, they don't know who we are. My dear friends, we are already God's children, though what we will be hasn't yet been seen. But we do know that when Christ returns, we will be like him, because we will see him as he truly is. This hope makes us keep ourselves holy, just as Christ is holy.

1 JOHN 3:1–3 CEV

*H*ave you ever looked into the mirror and thought, *I wish I had a new body?* Well, Christ has one reserved for you in heaven. That body is imperishable, undefiled, and will not fade away (1 Peter 1:3–4).

While we don't know when Jesus is coming again, we do know that our new bodies will coincide with this event. "When Christ, who is your life, appears, then you also will appear with him in glory" (Colossians 3:4 NIV).

Yet the gift of our new bodies is only one aspect of the Father's incredible love for His children. His love prompts His children to purify themselves just as He is pure (1 John 3:3). They also abide in Him and practice righteousness (3:6–7), for they have been born of God (3:9; John 3:7).

Father, thank You for the promise that I will one day receive a heavenly body. Forgive me when I am dissatisfied with the earthly body you have given me. Show me the best ways to take care of my health so that I can live a full life in service to You. Amen.

Harvest Kindness

*"If you love only those who love you, what reward is there for that?
Even corrupt tax collectors do that much."*

MATTHEW 5:46 NLT

Do you realize that we have golden opportunities to show love to others every single day? It's true! When that telemarketer interrupts your dinner and you're tempted to hang up right in that person's ear, don't do it. Show mercy and kindness. Or when you encounter rudeness when checking out at the grocery store, don't return rudeness with more rudeness. No, counter that evil with goodness.

Why? The Bible says we're supposed to do unto others as we would have them do unto us. If we'll discipline ourselves and show kindness when we want to react rudely, God will reward us. This is especially true when it comes to our children. Try it! The next time one of your kids gives you the "whatever" sign and blows you off for no reason, smile sweetly and say, "You are so precious to me. I love you." It won't be easy. Your flesh will want to scream, "Listen, kiddo, you'll not 'whatever' me and get away with it! I am your mother. So don't even go there with me!"

Make kindness a habit. You'll find that if you sow seeds of kindness, you'll reap a mighty harvest of kindness. Now that's the kind of crop I want in my life—how about you?

*Lord, help me to show love and kindness
to those who are unlovely and unkind. Amen.*

The Least of These

*The king will answer, "Whenever you did it for any of my people,
no matter how unimportant they seemed, you did it for me."*
MATTHEW 25:40 CEV

Some people act as if children are something to be tolerated, not cultivated. They are signed up for this, dropped off for that, and somehow, in the course of all of the activity, they are supposed to learn and grow into adults with a sense of thoughtful purpose. Do we think they'll teach themselves?

Jesus understood the potential of each child. He knew that their little hearts and minds were hungry for knowledge and truth. He knew that their training was an investment in the future of the kingdom of God.

We may never know the full scope of our impact on our own kids, but we are definitely part of God's plan for the development of their young lives. As a mother, you have the potential to bless a child's life forever.

And according to the Lord Himself, whatever you do for a child, you do for Him.

---

*Jesus, use me to shape the lives of my children for Your glory.
Help me to see these kids as a gift from You—never as a hindrance
to my adult pursuits. Please grant me Your wisdom and love. Amen.*

Blessings or Burdens?

"Let the children come to me. Don't stop them! For the Kingdom of God belongs to those who are like these children."
MARK 10:14 NLT

❀

"Did you get your homework done?"

"Clean your room!"

"Stop teasing your sister!"

"No, you cannot have potato chips for dinner."

"If I have to change one more diaper, I'm gonna scream."

Sound familiar?

Not exactly the picture-perfect family scenario you were hoping for—but this is reality.

Like all of us, Jesus had a busy schedule. Yet He took time for children. Think about it—the Lord of glory bounced kids on His lap! The disciples tried to shoo the children away. After all, there were more important matters to attend to, and they couldn't be bothered by giggling kids with runny noses.

Are we sometimes so caught up in "being Mom" that we forget to stop and enjoy the moments we have with our children? Would a potato chip dinner over a board game knock us out of the running for "Mom of the Year"?

Let's make sure our children know they're not a burden, but a blessing.

❀

Father God, what a blessing You have given me in my children. Teach me how to enjoy my time with them. Amen.

Reflecting God in Our Work

Whatever you do, work at it with all your heart,
as working for the Lord, not for human masters.
COLOSSIANS 3:23 NIV

Children are a reflection of their parents. When a mom and dad send their offspring out into the world, they can only hope that the reflection will be a positive one.

As believers, we are God's children. No one is perfect, and for this there is grace. However, we may be the only reflection of our heavenly Father that some will ever see. Our attitudes and actions on the job speak volumes to those around us. Although it may be tempting to do just enough to get by, we put forth our best effort when we remember we represent God to the world. A Christian's character on the job should be a positive reflection of the Lord.

This is true of our work at home as well. No one would disagree that daily chores are often monotonous, but we are called to face them with a cheerful spirit. God will give us the ability to do so when we ask Him.

Father, help me today to represent You well through my work.
I want to reflect Your love in all I do. Amen.

Be a Wise Builder

Every wise woman buildeth her house:
but the foolish plucketh it down with her hands.
PROVERBS 14:1 KJV

No matter the season of her life, no matter what house she is in, a woman should be about the business of building a home and a family.

While home building is the highest calling of womanhood, we sometimes turn aside from it, thinking the world offers something better. We sometimes think the world's view of personal achievement is better than God's view of submission and self-sacrifice.

Don't be fooled—real wisdom is found as we apply scripture to the many tasks of homemaking. Teaching kindness to a two-year-old is more difficult than teaching economic theory to graduate students, and explaining salvation to a preschooler is more challenging than convincing a bank to finance a business plan.

When done well, home building will yield rewards for many generations. When done thoughtlessly, generations suffer.

Let's not neglect this great task for the Lord.

Let us be wise builders.

Father, even though I know building a home is my most important job, sometimes I don't see the value. Let me labor in my home with diligence and grace, knowing it is truly my best work. Amen.

A Labor of Love

Therefore, my dear brothers and sisters, stand firm. Let nothing move you. Always give yourselves fully to the work of the Lord, because you know that your labor in the Lord is not in vain.

1 CORINTHIANS 15:58 NIV

"Cover your mouth!"

"Did you brush your teeth?"

"Don't talk with your mouth full!"

"No, you can*not* eat candy for breakfast."

To the casual observer, it may appear that our labor of love—with all of its dos, don'ts, and did yous—has been for naught. After all, how many times should one have to say, "Don't kick your sister!" before Bobby finally gets it? Apparently ninety-eight and counting.

And then there are the deeper issues of life. We teach our kids to treat mean people with kindness, to forgive when they would rather hold a grudge. They're hard lessons to learn, but our labor is not in vain. We have His Word on it.

Raising children to love and honor the Lord is tough work, but the key is never to give in to discouragement. Nothing we do for the Lord is ever wasted. . .even reminding little Bobby to stop kicking his sister!

Father God, as I raise my children to honor and respect You, You've promised that my labor is never wasted. What a promise to count on!

He Is the Answer

"Martha, Martha," the Lord answered, "you are worried and upset
about many things, but few things are needed—or indeed only one.
Mary has chosen what is better, and it will not be taken away from her."
Luke 10:41–42 niv

Do you remember when you were pregnant? In the midst of weird food cravings, swollen ankles, and raging hormones, you spent time dreaming of your baby. You wondered things like: "What will he or she look like?" "What will be his or her first words?" "Will he or she be healthy?" and "How will I ever care for a tiny little baby?"

Every mother worries. It seems like the natural thing to do. Most first-time moms worry that they won't be equipped with the appropriate parenting skills needed to be a good mom. Then the baby comes—and with it, a whole new set of worries. As the child grows, the worries grow, too. Sometimes, the worries can become almost suffocating.

When we feel overwhelmed with the worries that accompany motherhood, it's likely we've forgotten to figure God into the equation. With God, all things are possible—even raising good kids in a mixed-up world. God doesn't expect mothers to have all the answers, but He does expect us to go to Him for those answers. So, if worries are consuming your thoughts—go to God. He not only has the answers, He *is* the answer!

God, I trust You with my children
and I give You my worries. Amen.

Love Is All You Need

God is love. Whoever lives in love lives in God, and God in him.
This is how love is made complete among us.
1 JOHN 4:16–17 NIV

Remember that popular '70s song "Love Will Keep Us Together"?
Well, there's a lot of truth in that title, especially where our families are
concerned.

Life gets complicated, and families fall apart. It happens. It even
happens to Christian families. It may have happened in your own
family. But no matter what, love is the answer. When nothing else will,
love will keep your family together. Not the fair-weather kind of love,
but the God kind of love—an everlasting, unconditional love from
heaven.

So even if your teenager has left home or turned his back on God,
love will draw him back. Not the sermons you've preached nor the
rules you've enforced—only love will turn your situation around. Let
God's love live big in you. Let God's love be the superglue in your
family, binding you with one another for a lifetime. Live the love and
reap the results.

Father, I ask that Your love flow
through me to my children. Amen.

The House of Babel

"Come, let us go down and confuse their language so they will not understand each other." So the Lord scattered them from there over all the earth, and they stopped building the city. That is why it was called Babel.

GENESIS 11:7–9 NIV

Early in biblical history, the world's people spoke only one language. They wandered about, came to a plain in Babylonia, and settled there. Then they decided to build a tower, a religious symbol, to reach the sky. On top of this tower there was probably an altar on which human sacrifices were offered. In punishment, God responded by confounding their language.

Communication is a powerful tool. But it's often confounded, even in our homes. There are times when parents seem to speak a totally different language than their children! Thankfully, God can cut through all the miscommunication. He hears and understands what we're saying, and He speaks to us, too. God says, "I will instruct you and teach you in the way you should go; I will counsel you with my loving eye on you" (Psalm 32:8). But that requires listening as much as talking.

Lord, unstuff my ears and those of my children!
Help us to listen carefully to Your voice and to each other. Amen.

You Look Just Like. . .

For God knew his people in advance, and he chose
them to become like his Son, so that his Son would
be the firstborn among many brothers and sisters.

ROMANS 8:29 NLT

❋

amily resemblance. We all have some resemblance to our parents,
even if we never saw them due to death or adoption. It could be
physical, like the shape of our nose, or it could be in our mannerisms,
like the way we walk or laugh.

When others tell us how much our children look like us or act like
us, we generally respond by saying, "Thank you." For some reason,
such comments elicit pride in us.

It's much the same in our Christian experience. Once we've been
brought into the family of God, we begin to take on its defining
characteristics. Through the Holy Spirit, we are molded into the
image of Christ, sharing His mind-set and traits. Patience, kindness,
compassion, and the desire to please God gradually become part of
who we are.

Just as we enjoy the resemblance our own children bear toward us,
our heavenly Father wants His children to "look like" Him.

❋

Lord, please have Your way with me.
Cause me to bear the family resemblance. Amen.

Peanut Butter and Jelly

Better a dry crust eaten in peace than a
house filled with feasting—and conflict.

PROVERBS 17:1 NLT

❀

You've just cooked the perfect meal and are ready to sit down, relax, and eat. . . . But then the kids come to the table, bickering and pushing each other. You settle things down momentarily, then hear an under-the-table kick followed by a scream.

At this point, do you still feel like eating that wonderful meal? Proverbs 17 says it would be better for a family to dine on bread and water, in peace, than on a huge feast, when everyone is unhappy and fighting.

If you find yourself in the latter situation more often than not, maybe it's time for the bread and water. Instead of devoting time to an elaborate meal, just sit at the table together with a loaf of bread and jars of peanut butter and jelly. Talk, share, and prepare the evening meal together.

Your family will live through the night without a three-course dinner. And, just maybe, the extra time together around simpler fare will reap bountiful rewards of contented peace.

❀

Heavenly Father, please bring peace to my home. Calm the bickering and the strife. Unite us in You so that we can enjoy one another. Amen.

Power over the Plastic

Better is a little with the fear of the Lord,
than great treasure with trouble. Better is a dinner
of herbs where love is, than a fatted calf with hatred.
PROVERBS 15:16–17 NKJV

*M*any of us receive more mail from credit card companies than from our relatives! We toss the letters out, but dozens more materialize in our mailboxes with tempting offers.

The pressure mounts as children beg to go to Disney World. Teens sigh for jeans like those worn by popular kids, *the* jeans with perfect designer rips. Meanwhile, the car threatens to give up the ghost. *Sigh.* Parents feel so weary, so discouraged. Dinner at a restaurant without cardboard crowns or curly slides sounds wonderful! All they have to do is hand over the plastic and sign on the dotted line. . . .

God's Word comes to our rescue when we face little temptations that can add up to big trouble. Lovingly He reminds us that unrealistic expectations and overspending can destroy a family. Even macaroni and cheese—again!—with those we love tastes better than costly meals out that strain the budget and rob us of our peace.

Lord Jesus, thank You for Your concern in every
area of our lives. Help us as a family to live within
our means and enjoy the riches of a happy home. Amen.

Finding Balance

But the Lord said to her, "My dear Martha, you are worried and upset over all these details! There is only one thing worth being concerned about. Mary has discovered it, and it will not be taken away from her."
LUKE 10:41–42 NLT

With people in the house, needing to be fed, Martha jumped in to accomplish her tasks. Mary, on the other hand, chose to spend time in the presence of Jesus.

Because of Mary's choice, Martha had to do all the work by herself. She was even chastised for criticizing Mary. But if Martha hadn't done that work, who would have?

The two sisters from Bethany are a perfect example of the inner struggle that most women face daily. On one hand, we want to multitask and get things done. On the other hand, we crave rest, spiritual growth, and peace. The challenge is to blend the two into a healthy whole.

God has called us to good deeds, but not to stress and worry. Ask Him to show you the line.

Dear Lord, I want to do my part, like Martha—but, like Mary, I also need to be strong enough to say no, in order to have time with You. Please show me how to find that balance in my life. Amen.

See It and Believe It

❧

Are you focusing on the future, or are you having trouble seeing past the endless piles of dirty laundry that are in front of you right now? When today has so many worries, responsibilities, and obligations, it's difficult to be future minded. But we need to make a conscious effort. We need to let God stir up our faith. We need to start believing God for big things. We need to realize that even if the circumstances aren't so great today, God is bringing about a miracle in our future.

You see, no matter what you're dealing with today, God has a plan that will work things out better than you could ever imagine—if you'll just get your faith eyes in focus and become future minded. Ask God to help you change your focus.

The enemy doesn't want you to stand in faith for the fulfillment of your destiny. He doesn't want to see your children walking with God. He wants you to worry about all of the problems of today and forget about your future. Don't fall for the devil's plan. Focus on the future. See your children well and serving God. See your family happy and whole. See your dirty laundry washed, folded, and put away. Get a vision of victory today!

❧

Lord, help me get my faith eyes in focus
and looking toward the future. Amen.

Be Carefree

Cast all your anxiety on him because he cares for you.
1 PETER 5:7 NIV

*E*ver have one of those days? The alarm clock didn't go off. The kids were late for school. The dog threw up on the carpet. You spilled coffee down the front of your new white blouse. Ahhh! It's one of those "Calgon, take me away!" days, right?

But it doesn't have to be. No matter how many challenges you face today, you can smile in the face of aggravation. How? By casting your cares upon the Lord. That's what the Lord tells us to do in His Word, yet many of us feel compelled to take all of the cares upon ourselves. After all, we're mothers. We're fixers. We're the doers of the bunch. We wear five or six fedoras at a time—we can handle anything that comes our way, right?

Wrong! But God can. When the day starts to go south, cast your cares on Him. He wants you to! As mothers, we can handle a lot, but it's true what they say—Father really does know best. So give it to God. C'mon, you know you want to. . . .

Lord, help me to turn to You when my troubles seem too big to face alone and even when they don't. Help me to trust You with all of my cares. I love You, Lord. Amen.

Feeling the Squeeze

The eye can never say to the hand, "I don't need you."
The head can't say to the feet, "I don't need you."
1 CORINTHIANS 12:21 NLT

We've all heard the term "the sandwich generation," referring to midlifers coping with teenagers on one end and aging parents on the other. Somehow, calling it a sandwich sounds too easy. The in-between filling seems to fit comfortably, like ham and Swiss on rye. A more appropriate term would be "the squeeze generation." Picture peanut butter and jelly oozing out of squished white bread.

It is a challenging season of life, and we can't do it alone. And perhaps that is a great blessing to realize. God never meant for us to do it alone! He designed us to live in communities—family, friends, and church—that help meet one another's needs. "The body is a unit," Paul told the believers at Corinth, "though it is made up of many parts; and though all its parts are many, they form one body. So it is with Christ" (12:12 NIV).

There's nothing wrong with asking for help when you need it.

Lord, You promise never to leave us nor forsake us.
Thank You for providing helpers to come alongside of me. Amen.

Listening versus Talking

"My sheep listen to my voice;
I know them, and they follow me."

JOHN 10:27 NIV

❦

It has been said that the Lord gave us two ears and one mouth for a reason: we need to listen twice as much as we speak. However, talking seems to come easier for most of us. Our interaction with others becomes the model for our relationship with the Lord. We can become so busy talking to Him during our prayer time that we forget He has important wisdom to impart to us!

Jesus is our Good Shepherd. As His sheep, we have the ability to distinguish His voice. But are we taking the time to listen? It seems much of our prayer time is devoted to reciting our wish list to God. When we stop and think about it, doesn't God already know our needs before we utter one word? We need to learn to listen more instead of dominating the conversation. God is the One with the answers. He knows all things and possesses the wisdom we yearn for.

Learning to listen takes time. Do not be afraid to sit in silence before the Lord. Read His Word. He will speak softly to your heart. He will impart truth to your hungry soul. He will guide you on the path you should take. Listen.

❦

Dear Lord, help me learn how to listen and distinguish Your voice.
Grant me time to be silent in Your presence.
Speak to my heart so that I may follow You. Amen.

Establishing a Vision

Where there is no vision, the people perish.
PROVERBS 29:18 KJV

Cookbooks without pictures aren't much fun. Simple words on a page typically don't move us to culinary pursuits. But if that decadent New York–style cheesecake recipe is actually pictured, we may *run* to the kitchen!

Moms, too, need an image of what we're trying to accomplish. What do we see as the end result of all our efforts? What does success in our family, our parenting, our career, our spiritual life look like? We need a vision. Without it, we'll probably walk aimlessly through piles of laundry, stacks of bills, and grocery store aisles.

With a clear mental image of the future, we can visualize where all the hard work of parenthood is taking us—and see, in our mind's eye, the big picture of what God is creating in us and in the lives of our children.

Ask God to give you a vision of your ultimate destination. It'll make worlds of difference in your day-to-day labors.

Father God, allow me to see the vision You have established for my family—embed it into my heart and mind. Amen.

So Little Time

Come, my children, and listen to me,
and I will teach you to fear the LORD.
PSALM 34:11 NLT

If you could only teach your children ten things before you died, what would you share? Would you teach them to stand up for who they are in Christ Jesus? Would you teach them self-defense? Would you teach them good manners? Would you teach them to give to others? Would you teach them to treat others with respect? Would you teach them how to be a friend?

It's a tough call, isn't it? There are so many things we want to impart to our kids. We want to save them from making all of the stupid mistakes that we made. While we can't protect them from every mistake, we can put them on the road to success and happiness.

We can make the most of every opportunity to teach them about the nature of God—God the Healer, God the Provider, God the Savior, God the Deliverer, God the Great I Am! There are chances every day to share little lessons with our children. Ask the Lord to help you identify those opportunities so that you can take advantage of each one.

Lord, help me to share Your love with my children
each day. And, Lord, help me to take advantage of
every opportunity to teach my kids about You. Amen.

Turn Your Ear to Wisdom

For the LORD grants wisdom! From his mouth come knowledge and understanding. He grants a treasure of common sense to the honest. He is a shield to those who walk with integrity. He guards the paths of the just and protects those who are faithful to him.

PROVERBS 2:6–8 NLT

❧

*E*very family has at least one relative who cannot get his act together. (Meanwhile the rest of us scratch our heads and wonder how he can miss the obvious, every single time.) It's as though these people have to fall in every pothole in the street because it never occurs to them to go down a different road.

Are you smiling yet? Is someone in particular coming clearly into focus? Now hold that thought.

God's Word says wisdom is truly a gift since it comes from the mouth of God, from the very words He speaks. And all God's words have been written down for us, through the inspiration of the Holy Spirit. Therefore, those who refuse to accept God's guidance, who refuse to ask for His wisdom—those hapless relatives, perhaps—will never see the light of reality.

Know that if you hold fast to the precepts contained in the Bible, you will walk in integrity. Instead of gravitating toward potholes, your feet will be planted on the straight and narrow road.

❧

Lord, I can't change my relatives, but I can change myself. So if my head is the one peeking out of the pothole, please pull me out!

Be Happy

A heart at peace gives life to the body.
PROVERBS 14:30 NIV

Are you at peace with the person God made you to be?

If you don't have peace within yourself, you'll never have peace with other people. God could send you another mom to be the friend you've been praying for, but if you're not at peace with yourself, that relationship won't work. You've got to be happy with who God made you to be before you can experience healthy relationships.

If you're focused on your imperfections and are constantly wishing you were someone else, you're allowing the devil to steal your peace and replace it with wrong thinking. Don't get caught in that trap. That's a miserable way to live. Learn to celebrate the person God made you to be.

The devil will try to convince you that you're a weak worm of the dust. He'll try to get you thinking wrong about yourself. But you need to declare out loud, "I am a child of the Most High King, and He thinks I'm great."

You may not be happy with every aspect of yourself, but you need to be happy about the basic person God created you to be. When you start practicing that mind-set, your peace will return. And that's a great way to live!

*Lord, I pray that Your peace overtakes me today.
Change my wrong thinking. Amen.*

A Wonderful Life

My heart panteth, my strength faileth me:
as for the light of mine eyes, it also is gone from me.
PSALM 38:10 KJV

❀

*E*mma was as old as the hills. She had mothered a dozen children, tended a hundred grandchildren, and no one knew how many great- and great-great grandchildren. She worked every day of the first ninety years of her life; then she decided to rest. In her 103rd year, she lost her sight, and two years later she was confined to a wheelchair. For a while, she was resentful of losing her faculties, but in time she accepted it. After all, hadn't she lived more than a full life? Hadn't God given her more family than any one woman had a right to have? When all was said and done, Emma had had a wonderful life, and a few inconveniences at the end certainly weren't going to get her down.

We have two simple options when afflictions strike. We can moan about our fate and give up, or we can face it boldly and make the best of it. God grants us the power to become more than conquerors, if we will only choose to use it.

❀

Lord, I know there will be times when my strength fails and my will is drained. At those times, fill my heart with Your will and power. Make me a fighter, Lord. Amen.

Eat Your Fill

There is a time for everything, and a season for every activity under the heavens. . .a time to embrace and a time to refrain from embracing.

ECCLESIASTES 3:1, 5 NIV

❀

Author Carol Kuykendall tells a story of stopping at a roadside fruit stand after dropping her son off at college. As she filled a bag with peaches, the cashier commented, "Better eat your fill of those peaches. When they're gone, you won't miss them so much."

Carol felt the cashier had given her wisdom that applied to more than peaches. She went home, cleared her calendar of all but necessities for the year, and became more available for her daughter still living at home.

When her daughter left for college, they were closer than ever, and she wasn't burdened by regret over missed moments.

Wise old Solomon observed a certain pattern that God Himself had set into motion: seasons of nature, seasons of change in our lives. Solomon could see the big picture, understanding that we have little control over many things. Instead of fighting that rhythm, we can embrace it, acknowledging that seasons are part of God's plan for our lives.

❀

Lord, help us to see our lives with a long view. Give us Your peace as we face our future, knowing You are in control. Amen.

Reap Joy

"Give, and it will be given to you: good measure,
pressed down, shaken together, and running over."
LUKE 6:38 NKJV

Did you know that God wants you to be happy? He desires for you to live life to its fullest. It doesn't matter that you might be elbow deep in diapers and carpools right now—you can still enjoy life!

One of the main ways you can guarantee joy in your life is by living to give. You see, true happiness comes when we give of ourselves to others—our spouses, our children, our extended family, our church, our community, and our friends. As moms, we're sort of trained to be givers. We give up our careers, many times, to become full-time moms. We give up a full night's sleep to feed our babies. We give up sports cars for minivans and SUVs to accommodate our families. In fact, we'd give our lives for our children.

But sometimes our attitudes are less than joyful in all of our giving, right? Well, rejoice today. God promises to multiply back to you everything that you give. When you step out in faith, you open a door for God to move on your behalf. It's the simple principle of sowing and reaping. And as mothers, we are super sowers. So get ready for a super-huge harvest!

Lord, help me to live to give with the right attitude.
I love You. Amen.

Praise Him in Song

Take a psalm, and bring hither the timbrel,
the pleasant harp with the psaltery.
PSALM 81:2 KJV

❀

*B*eth was different when she was singing. Somehow the pressures
of the world disappeared when the music filled her head and heart.
Her whole life felt somehow lighter, brighter, when she lifted her voice
in praise through song. Music was the best expression of who she was
and what she believed. Music made God real to Beth.

Music is a universal language. Every culture has its music, and it
is revered as one of the finest arts. Music brings people together and
can move us closer to God. God loves music and the spirit from which
music springs. The quality is not nearly as important as the intention
of the heart. Sing out to God, and He will bless you richly.

❀

Music touches my heart in a special way, Lord. Speak to me
through the beauty of music. Touch me day by day. Amen.

Choosing Wisely

Our mouths were filled with laughter.
PSALM 126:2 NIV

❧

Amanda stared glumly at the rock-hard turkey parked on the kitchen counter. She'd miscalculated defrosting time; it was now Thanksgiving morning, and the entrée of honor was still obstinately ossified.

The twenty-two-pound bird was too large for the microwave, so she tried the blow-dryer. Warm air only deflected into her face. Dunking the bird in a warm bathtub merely cooled the water down, and whacking the turkey with a hammer only intensified her budding headache.

Lunch was at noon. Guests would soon be arriving. What to do?

We women often plan perfect family events, only to find out how imperfectly things can turn out. Our reactions to these surprise glitches can make or break the event for everyone present. Mom's foul mood sucks the joy from the room.

The Bible says that Sarah laughed at the most unexpected, traumatic time of her life—when God announced that she would have a baby at the age of ninety (Genesis 18:12). At this unforeseen turn of events, she could either laugh, cry, or run away screaming.

She chose to laugh.

❧

Lord, give us an extra dollop of grace and peace
to laugh about unexpected dilemmas that pop up.
And to remember that our reaction is a choice. Amen.

Joy Is Jesus

Though you do not see [Jesus] now, you trust him; and you rejoice with a glorious, inexpressible joy. The reward for trusting him will be the salvation of your souls.

1 PETER 1:8–9 NLT

As children we find joy in the smallest things: a rose in bloom, a ladybug at rest, the ripples a pebble makes when dropped in water. Then somewhere between pigtails and pantyhose, our joy wanes and eventually evaporates in the desert of difficulties.

But when we find Jesus, "all things become new" as the Bible promises, and once again, we view the world through a child's eyes.

We learn that God's joy begins with the seed of God's Word planted in our hearts. Suddenly, our hearts spill over with joy, knowing that God loves and forgives us and that He is in complete control of our lives. We have joy because we know this world is not our permanent home and a mansion awaits us in glory.

Joy comes as a result of whom we trust, not in what we have. Joy is Jesus.

Dear Jesus, thank You for giving me the joy of my salvation. Knowing You surpasses anything and everything else the world offers. Amen.

The Promise of Joy

Weeping may endure for a night,
but joy cometh in the morning.

PSALM 30:5 KJV

Have you experienced suffering? Perhaps you are hurting even now. Tough times are a reality for all of us.

The psalmist David was well acquainted with hardship. Although he was known as a man after God's own heart, at times David was pursued by his enemies and forced to run for his life. He also lived with the consequences of committing murder and adultery long after receiving God's forgiveness. But God is faithful, and suffering is temporary. This is a promise we can claim, as David did, when facing difficulty or depression.

As believers, we can find joy in the Lord even as certain trials persist in our lives. All suffering will end one day when we meet Jesus. The Bible assures us that in heaven there will be no tears.

Your loving heavenly Father has not forgotten you. You may feel that relief will never come, but take courage. It will.

God, where there is anguish in my life, may Your joy enter in.
I ask for grace to face my trials, knowing that in time
You will replace weeping with joy. Amen.

Food, Glorious Food

I am convinced, being fully persuaded in the Lord Jesus,
that nothing is unclean in itself. But if anyone regards
something as unclean, then for that person it is unclean.
ROMANS 14:14 NIV

🌸

A wise person once said that you couldn't spell *diet* without d–i–e. That's pretty much how many of us feel about cutting back on those wonderfully bad-for-us entrees and desserts we all love so much.

The apostle Paul writes in Romans that no food is unclean in itself—but if a person regards something as unclean, she shouldn't eat it. At the time, Paul was talking about food sacrificed to idols, but today he could just as easily be referring to fast foods and sweets. We know those foods aren't good for us, but we sure enjoy eating them.

Good foods, though, don't have to be unpleasant. And they're definitely better for God's temple—our bodies.

Start small. Stock the fridge or cupboards with fruit, low-fat yogurt, and other healthy snacks. Avoid the temptation to stop at a fast-food chain for lunch. Or, if you must eat quickly, choose a salad instead of a burger—and skip the fries entirely.

Your body—and maybe even your kids—will thank you later.

🌸

Dear Lord, help me to choose healthy foods for my children
and myself. I know that no food is "unclean" on its own, but
eating the wrong things could harm the body You have given me. Amen.

Time Clocks

Is not the LORD your God with you?
and hath he not given you rest on every side?
1 CHRONICLES 22:18 KJV

❀

The time clock is a wonderful invention. You clock in and (here is the best part) you clock out! While we're "on the clock," we're aware that our time is not our own. Whether cooking for a hungry throng of customers, typing on a keyboard, or emptying trash, for a set time we must do another's bidding. Then we go home, off the clock at last.

At home, there is no time clock. No way to "punch out" for the day. Our duties seem endless: picking up dry cleaning, rushing to a soccer game, folding the millionth load of laundry, trying to find an interesting way to use hamburger *again*, reading to the kids, helping with homework. . . Where's the time clock to put an end to this work?

God promises to give His people rest. The laundry will be there tomorrow. We can occasionally live with cereal for dinner. The vacuuming can wait for the weekend. Algebra will always be hard.

Slow down. Rest. Catch your breath. Allow God to renew you. You have His permission to clock out for the day.

❀

*Father God, teach me how to slow down. There are so
many pressing needs, yet I know I must find a way
to clock out for my day. Enable me to rest in You. Amen.*

A Disciplined Mom

The wise woman builds her house,
But the foolish pulls it down with her hands.

PROVERBS 14:1 NKJV

❋

Being a lazy parent creates more work! Shortcuts often seem easier, but taking the time to make the tough choices now and to consistently discipline our children will prevent bigger problems down the road.

Compare lackadaisical parenting shortcuts to the effects of a poor diet. One bag of potato chips won't kill you. But a bag of chips, every day, over a period of years, will certainly cause trouble. The same is true in our jobs as mothers.

Lazy choices return negative effects over time—effects that can devastate our homes. The trouble may go unnoticed for some time. But when we realize the problems, it can be too late.

Determine now to make wise decisions, every day. Exercise simple, daily disciplines in your parenting. Make a commitment to consistency. Maintain your commitment to those daily disciplines, lest one poor choice lead to another—and you begin to tear down your home with your own hands.

The wise woman builds her house.

❋

Lord, let me honor You by my discipline in my daily responsibilities. Help me to consistently build up my household rather than tear it down. Please show me what You would have me do and then give me the strength to do it. Amen.

Belly Laughs

All the days of the oppressed are wretched,
but the cheerful heart has a continual feast.
PROVERBS 15:15 NIV

Do you know how to relax? Have you built a time for laughter into your schedule?

Maybe that sounds silly and unimportant with the demands of motherhood caving in on you. But it's not! In fact, relaxation and fun are vital to your health—and, by extension, the health of your family. We may face challenges, but as Proverbs reminds us, we can have a continual feast regardless of circumstances. Don't wait for laughter to find you—seek it out!

Find a clean comedy show to loosen up. Maybe get into a tickling match with the kids. Perhaps it's as simple as scheduling a popcorn and movie night with the kids to melt away the day's pressure.

A good laugh is health to our bones and gives our kids permission to lighten up, too. Do it now—not when life is in perfect order. Our families need to see us loosen up and enjoy ourselves now and then.

Heavenly Father, You are a God of laughter and enjoyment.
Why does it seem frivolous to giggle with my children?
Enable me to have a continual feast regardless of my circumstances. Amen.

Clap Your Hands!

*Clap your hands, all you nations; shout to
God with cries of joy. For the LORD Most High
is awesome, the great King over all the earth!...*

PSALM 47:1–2 NIV

In 1931, German theologian Dietrich Bonhoeffer spent a year at a seminary in New York City. While there, he was introduced to a church in Harlem. Astounded, then delighted, at the emotion expressed in worship, he returned to Germany with recordings of gospel music tucked in his suitcase. Bonhoeffer knew that the worship he observed was authentic and pleasing to God.

King David would have loved gospel music! Many of the psalms were meant to be sung loudly and joyfully. David appointed four thousand professional musicians—playing cymbals, trumpets, rams' horns, tambourines, harps, and lyres—for temple worship. We can imagine they would have rocked the roofs off of our modern-day church services!

Dancing was a part of worship in David's day, too. David angered his wife, Michal, with his spontaneous dance in the street, as the Ark of the Covenant was returned to Jerusalem (1 Chronicles 15:29). The world, in David's viewpoint, couldn't contain the delight that God inspires. Neither could he!

How often do we worship God with our whole heart? Do our children ever see us burst forth in a song of praise? Have they witnessed us clapping our hands and lifting them up high? Probably not often enough. Let's try that today!

O Lord, great is Your name and worthy of praise!

Ideal Place

For you see your calling, brethren, that not many wise
according to the flesh, not many mighty, not many noble,
are called. But God has chosen the foolish things of the
world to put to shame the wise, and God has chosen the weak
things of the world to put to shame the things which are mighty.

1 CORINTHIANS 1:26–27 NKJV

Once my life is running smoothly. . .
If I didn't have toddlers underfoot. . .
As soon as I get this anger problem under control. . .
When I get enough money. . .
As soon as I (fill in the blank). . .then I can be used by God.

We are *where* we are, *when* we are, because our Father chose us for
such a time as this. Our steps are ordered by Him. Whether He has
called us to teach a Sunday school class, pray with other moms, lead a
Bible study, or sing in the choir—we need not wait for the ideal time
and place to serve Him. The only "ideal" is where you are right now.

God delights in using His people—right in the middle of all that
appears crazy and wrong and hopeless. *Now* is the time to serve God,
not next week or next year or when things get better. He wants our
cheerful, obedient service right in the midst of—even in spite of—our
difficult circumstances.

Father, help me see that there is no "ideal" place or circumstance to serve
You. You can, and will, use me right where I am. Thank You
that I do not have to have it all together to be used by You. Amen.

The Undercover Mission Trip

If I rise on the wings of the dawn, if I settle on the far side of the sea,
even there your hand will guide me, your right hand will hold me fast.
PSALM 139:9–10 NIV

Lindsey had to beg her mom to go on a summer mission trip.
"Please, Mom," Lindsey pleaded. "I really believe God wants me to go."

It wasn't that Lindsey's mom wanted to hold her back or interfere
with God's plans, but Lindsey was considering a Third World country
where Christianity was illegal! For eight long weeks, there could be no
phone calls, e-mails, or letters because they might jeopardize the safety
of those on the trip. The undercover mission trip.

After praying, Lindsey's mom agreed to let her go. But it still wasn't
easy. She missed her daughter. She worried about Lindsey, prayed to
hand those worries over to God, and often snatched them back again.

At midsummer, a friend called unexpectedly. "Would you believe
that my nephew is on that same mission trip as Lindsey? And his sister
had gone on that trip, a few years ago."

"And she returned home," Lindsey's mom asked, "safe and sound?"

"Safe and sound," her friend reassured her.

As Lindsey's mom hung up the phone, she almost laughed. God
had delivered just the right encouragement at just the right moment.

Lord God, You are faithful even when I am not.
And You are faithful to my children, even when I have doubts.
I praise You for Your providential care today. Amen.

Thousands of Millions

And they blessed Rebekah, and said unto her,
Thou art our sister, be thou the mother of thousands of millions,
and let thy seed possess the gate of those which hate them.
GENESIS 24:60 KJV

How would you have responded if, prior to your wedding, your family members said to you, "We hope you are blessed with thousands of millions of children"? You likely would have laughed and told them to keep their comments to themselves, and they would have thought it a joke as well. Rebekah's family was sincere, though. In her day, children were considered a blessing from God. The more children a woman had, the more blessed she was. Of course, Rebekah's family didn't expect her to give birth to that many children. They were simply asking God to bless her new family.

Children are God's blessing to you. Whether you have one child or many, you have a unique opportunity to influence the world. As they grow, they will have the chance to witness to those you might never meet, and the process will continue.

Rebekah only bore two children—nowhere close to "thousands of millions." But one of her sons was Jacob—the father of Christ's bloodline. Rebekah was blessed indeed, and so are you. That's something to keep in mind as you go through your day.

Dear Lord, You have blessed me with beautiful
children and a special opportunity to influence many people.
Help me take this responsibility to heart. Amen.

A Pattern Worth Repeating

Know therefore that the LORD your God is God; he is the faithful God, keeping his covenant of love to a thousand generations of those who love him and keep his commandments.

DEUTERONOMY 7:9 NIV

We all know that patterns repeat in families, even to the "third and fourth generation" (Exodus 20:5). We worry over negative patterns, like abuse and divorce, that have hurt our children the same way they hurt us. We long to replace those negative patterns with godly, joyful living.

God wants that for our families, as well. He encourages parents with a God-sized promise, the kind every mother wants for her family but thinks is impossible.

Think beyond a legacy for our grandchildren and great-grandchildren. God's vision extends far past that. He will show "love for a *thousand lifetimes*" (emphasis added). Taken literally, at twenty-five years times one thousand, it endures for twenty-five thousand years—longer than people have lived on the earth.

God takes our hands and says, "Love Me. Obey Me. I will show love to your family as long as you have descendants on the earth." And when we demonstrate our love for God by doing what He says, we guarantee His faithfulness and love to generations yet unborn, until the Lord returns to take us home.

That's a legacy worth passing on.

Heavenly Father, I praise You that You will be faithful to my children and their children after them. I pray that they also will love You and obey You.

Best Dressed Secret

*Those who look to him are radiant;
their faces are never covered with shame.*

PSALM 34:5 NIV

Little Orphan Annie, dressed in threadbare hand-me-down clothes, gets the other girls in the orphanage to sing along with her. "You're never fully dressed without a smile."

We could all learn a lesson from Annie. Maybe we need to add it to our morning checklist: make breakfast, pack lunches, get children ready for school, apply makeup, and, oh yes—put on a smile.

Smiling does the heart good. Age will not dim our smiles, and they announce our happiness to the world.

But we're not happy, we might argue. We worry when there's too much month left at the end of the paycheck. Our children's misbehavior weighs us down. We long for adult companionship and suffer loneliness. We battle anger, regret, and bitterness over our life situation.

Maybe we could choose another word and say we're joyful. Unlike happiness, joy depends on God rather than our circumstances. As the psalmist points out, God never disappoints anyone who comes to Him for help. He may not help us in quite the way we expect, but He will always give us exactly what we need.

When we wear a happy face despite our circumstances, we may find that our inward spirit changes to match the outward smile.

*Dear Lord, let our smiles come from the inside out.
Our circumstances change, but You never do. Thank You, Lord!*

The Gift of Friends

*Two are better than one, because they have a good return for their
labor: If either of them falls down, one can help the other up.
But pity anyone who falls and has no one to help them up.*

ECCLESIASTES 4:9–10 NIV

As our children grow, we want good things—including good
friends—for them. Many of us have been praying for a spouse for our
child while our kid's still in diapers. We meet our kids' friends, and
often the parents of those friends, to be sure our kids are surrounding
themselves with positive influences.

Sometimes, though, we forget that adults have a similar need for
good friends. Moms especially would benefit from that one special
friend who will be there, no matter what. Maybe it's someone to shop
with or borrow a sweater from, or maybe it's that trusted friend who
will answer the phone in the middle of the night when little Jillian has
a high fever or we simply need to vent our frustrations.

Jesus is our helper and our hope, undoubtedly. But often He works
through sincere and trusted friends—especially that one special friend
for whom the blessings are mutual.

*Lord, sometimes I feel lonely and in desperate need of a friend
who will be honest with me and yet not judge me. . . someone who
will send me a note on Valentine's Day or find time to join
me for coffee or a movie. Please bless me with one true friend,
a gift from You, to fill some of the void I feel in my life. Amen.*

What Is Prayer?

O my God, I cry in the day time, but thou hearest not;
and in the night season, and am not silent.

PSALM 22:2 KJV

❊

Prayer is a tricky thing. It was never meant as a "gimme" list by which we can get things from God. It is not a gripe time to vent frustrations and woes. It is not a time to show off our piety. Rather, it is a time to draw close to God in order to be open to His will and guidance. So often we feel that God is not listening because we don't get what we ask for. We want results immediately, and we decide beforehand what we will accept as an answer and what we will not. Who says we get to make the rules? The Lord hears us, and He is true to answer us, but He always measures His responses according to His divine wisdom. He knows what is best for us, even when it doesn't agree with what we want. It is natural and human to doubt the Lord sometimes. He understands that. Just don't give up. The Lord breaks through our desert spots to comfort us when we cry.

❊

Lift me, Lord, into Your loving arms.
Grace me with the sweet memory of Your care,
that I might never doubt You in times of trial. Amen.

Unconditional Love

*"As bad as you are, you still know how to give good gifts
to your children. But your heavenly Father is even more
ready to give good things to people who ask."*
MATTHEW 7:11 CEV

❋

Whether you gave birth or adopted, do you remember the first time you laid eyes on your child? Their tiny features instantly enraptured your heart. Right there, on the spot, you were hooked. This parent-child bond, so powerful as to forever alter your life, also gave you a glimpse of unconditional love.

What happens to that bond when this little bundle of joy gets a few years older—and breaks your treasured vase or gets mud on your new beige carpet? Or when, as a teenager, your child shatters your heart with hurtful words and rebellious acts?

Do we tell our children, "You've crossed the line one too many times. I don't love you anymore"? The idea is absurd, isn't it?

Yet how often do we fear that our heavenly Father will react that way with *His* children? If we—imperfect as we are—have the capacity to show compassion, love, and mercy to our children, why would our Father in heaven show us any less?

❋

*Father, please open my eyes to the love
and devotion You have for me. Thank You!*

Love in Action

Dear children, let us not love with words
or speech but with actions and in truth.
1 JOHN 3:18 NIV

*S*aying "I love you" to our children is very important. They need to hear those words on a daily basis. But we also need to *show* that we love our children. Have you ever really thought about the common expression "Actions speak louder than words"? There's a lot of truth to that saying.

While it's easy to say "I love you," it's not so easy to show our love all the time. That's why another expression, "Talk is cheap," is used so often. As moms, we need to find ways to back up our "I love yous" every single day. In other words, walk the talk.

Make a conscious effort today to do something special for your children—something out of the ordinary. Leave them little love notes. Make them a special pancake breakfast and serve it by candlelight for added fun. Plan a family night out at one of their favorite places. Just find a unique way to show your kids how much you adore them. Ask God to help you in this area. He will. After all, the Bible says that God is love. He is the expert in showing love.

Heavenly Father, help me to show Your love to
my family on a daily basis. I love You. Amen.

His Wonderful Works

I will praise thee, O Lord, with my whole heart;
I will shew forth all thy marvellous works.

PSALM 9:1 KJV

Audrey loved the little children, and they dearly loved her. She would walk with them through the gardens and fields, showing them all the wonders of nature. She would sit with them for hours and tell them stories. She would read to them from her Bible then explain what she had read. She would remind the children of all the good things God could do. For the main part of her life, Audrey taught little children the reality of God.

To be truly in love with God is a consuming passion. We can't wait to tell the world of the wonderful truth we know. The Spirit of God enters in, and our lives are never the same again. Praise the Lord with your whole heart, and show forth all His wonderful works.

Each new day brings new wonders to my attention.
Thank You, O Lord, for creating such a beautiful
world with so many miracles to behold. Amen.

Meeting My Needs

*And my God will meet all your needs according
to the riches of his glory in Christ Jesus.*
PHILIPPIANS 4:19 NIV

Jillian strapped her two small girls into their car seats then settled
into the driver's seat. She glanced at the gas gauge, its needle pointing
frighteningly close to EMPTY. Jillian had to visit the store for milk,
bread, and diapers. How she could pay for those and still find enough
to cover the phone bill was anyone's guess. *God*, Jillian cried silently, *I
need Your help.*

Rest assured, moms—God hears our silent cries. While He never
promised to meet our wants or desires, He does promise to meet our
needs. That great new pair of black slingbacks in the shoe store window
may not qualify as a need in God's sight. But if we sincerely ask His
help, with a thankful heart, God miraculously covers us with His
riches. We find, somehow, that our needs are met. After all, He owns
the cattle on a thousand hills. And that's a lot of shoe leather.

Though we may not immediately appreciate *how* He does it, God
always comes through for us.

*Dear Lord, at times I find myself in need with bills that
need to be paid and cupboards that are bare. Please do a
miraculous work and cover me today and every day.
Your Word says You will meet my needs, so I put my
faith in You and stand firmly on Your Word. Thank You.*

A Mother's Love

This is how we know what love is: Jesus Christ laid down his life for us.
And we ought to lay down our lives for our brothers and sisters.

1 JOHN 3:16 NIV

❀

Recovering from surgery, a young boy reclined on the family sofa. As he described his anxiety leading up to the operation—and the pain following—his mother told him, "Son, I hate to see you suffer. If I could have taken your place, I would have."

The boy responded, "You must love me a lot to be willing to do that."

How that story echoes the Father's heart toward His children. He not only wanted to spare us agonizing, eternal pain, He actually bore the pain on our behalf. Suffering for us, taking our punishment. . . but not because we're so good or deserving. No—simply and purely because He loves us.

If we as moms are capable of such overwhelming compassion for our children, how much more does our heavenly Father care for us? God offers us the ultimate example of selfless love and infinite wisdom. And He'll help us with both in our own families.

❀

Father God, thank You for leaving us such an example
of love and selflessness. When I am weak and tired, grant
me a heart of patience and compassion for my own children. Amen.

Three Days without a Miracle

So the people grumbled against Moses,
saying "What are we to drink?"

EXODUS 15:24 NIV

❀

The Israelites were thirsty. Really, really thirsty. Their tongues felt thick, and their eyes burned under the glare of the hot sun.

They had been wandering in the desert for three days without water, and they were about to snap. Could anyone blame them? They did what people do when under stress. They blamed their leader. "Moses!" they complained. "It's all your fault!"

In reality, the Israelites had gone three days without a miracle. A few days prior, the Lord had parted the Red Sea, allowing the Israelites to escape, then closed it up again to drown the pursuing Egyptian army. Just three days ago! How had they forgotten God's just-in-time provision?

Moses didn't forget. His first response was to turn to God. "Then Moses cried out to the LORD, and the LORD showed him a piece of wood. He threw it into the water, and the water became sweet" (15:25).

God held the answer to the Israelites' basic needs. He responded to Moses' prayer immediately, as if He had just been waiting.

What if we turned to God immediately with our basic needs, instead of waiting until the thirst set in? What if we remembered His faithfulness before, or better still, instead of, panicking? Most likely, we would have our sweet water sooner.

❀

Lord, You are the supplier to my every need.
Thank You for Your faithfulness.

The Treasures of Wisdom

And the Child grew and became strong in spirit,
filled with wisdom; and the grace of God was upon Him.
LUKE 2:40 NKJV

What was Jesus like as a child? Did Mary and Joseph ever have cause to scold Him? As a toddler, did Jesus ever stick His hand in the fire? Or did He ever poke His baby brother to make him scream?

The Gospel of Luke is our only glimpse into Jesus' childhood. Our first peek into those years, from Luke 2, indicates that after Mary and Joseph returned to Galilee, Jesus grew, became strong, and was filled with wisdom.

Now fast-forward a few years. Jesus is twelve, a significant year in a Jewish boy's life—because He is now a man. With His parents, Jesus has traveled to Jerusalem for the Passover. After the weeklong festival, Mary and Joseph head home—only to discover, somewhere down the road, that Jesus is not among their group. Back they hurry to Jerusalem, fearing the worst. After three frantic days, they find Jesus calmly discussing theology in the temple. It almost seems as if the temple was the last place Joseph and Mary thought to search!

Luke closes this vignette with another description of Jesus' development: He "grew in wisdom and stature, and in favor with God and men" (2:52 NIV).

Does wisdom top the list of our goals for our children? Or is it stuffed underneath other hopes—for self-reliance, physical protection, or good grades? God Himself treasures wisdom—that one quality appears twice in the limited record of Jesus' childhood.

Lord, may my children commit themselves
to a lifelong search for Your wisdom. Amen.

Speak Kind Words of Love

A gentle answer turns away wrath,
but a harsh word stirs up anger.
PROVERBS 15:1 NIV

The young boy walked slowly into the kitchen. Head low, hands behind his back, he whispered, "Momma, I'm sorry."

She glared at the boy and said sharply, "What did you do?"

"I broke it," he said, showing her what he was hiding in his hand. It was a toy from a fast-food kids' meal that she had lovingly given to him just a few hours before. "I didn't mean to make you mad."

She saw the grief in her son's eyes and pulled him into her arms. "It's okay, baby," she said gently. "I'm not mad. But I am sorry—I shouldn't have yelled at you." Taking the broken toy, she said, "I think I can fix this if you'll help me. Would you go get the glue?"

The boy jumped up with a smile.

Ever been there? How often do we snap at our children when a kind word or a hug is what they really need? Today, let's plan ahead for such moments. When it seems like the kids are doing something wrong, first take a deep breath. Let go of the frustrations and remember that your children are still learning—not only from their mistakes but from your reactions as well. Then speak kind words of love.

Heavenly Father, help me show my children Your loving-kindness in all things. When correction is necessary, help me discipline from a heart of compassion. Amen.

The Early Hours

My voice shalt thou hear in the morning, O LORD; in the
morning will I direct my prayer unto thee, and will look up.
PSALM 5:3 KJV

The sun had just begun to climb into the sky, and the dew shone
brightly on the field below. Though not ordinarily a morning person,
Ann always loved those special times when she rose in time to see the
sunrise. *On mornings like this, who could doubt that there is a God?* Ann's
heart filled with a joy beyond words, and nothing could remove that
joy during the day. Taking a Bible, she went to a clearing to sit and to
read and to pray.

God gives us special times in order that we might find joy and
that we might find Him. He has created a glorious world, and He has
freely given it to us. The early quiet of the day is a beautiful time to
encounter the Lord. Give Him your early hours, and He will give you
all the blessings you can hold.

I raise my voice to You in the morning, Lord.
Help me to appreciate Your new day and use it to the fullest.
Open my eyes to the splendor of all Your creation. Amen.

Solid Ground

Great peace have they who love your law,
and nothing can make them stumble.
PSALM 119:165 NIV

𝒟id you know that God's Word contains approximately seven thousand promises in its pages? It has promises to cover any circumstance or problem that you'll ever encounter. If you're ill and need God's healing touch, the Word says, "By his wounds you have been healed" (1 Peter 2:24). If you're struggling financially, the Bible says, "My God will meet all your needs according to his glorious riches in Christ Jesus" (Philippians 4:19). If your teenagers are rebelling against you and God, the Word says, "But from everlasting to everlasting the LORD's love is with those who fear him, and his righteousness with their children's children" (Psalm 103:17).

No matter what is going on in your life today, God has got you covered. If you can find a promise in His Word, you have something solid to stand on and build your faith upon. Aren't you thankful for that today? God's Word has all of the answers, and we have access to those answers twenty-four hours a day. We live in a country that enjoys religious freedom, so we can even read His promises in public. Praise God for His promises today.

Thank You, Lord, for Your Word. I praise
You for the many promises contained in its pages. Amen.

The Discipline Dilemma

LORD. . .your laws are righteous, and in faithfulness you have afflicted
me. . . . Before I was afflicted I went astray, but now I obey your word.

PSALM 119:75, 67 NIV

Let's face it: we want our children to rely on us, to like us, to want to
be with us more than anyone else.

But the I-want-my-kids-to-like-me syndrome can cause some
parents to recoil from even the thought of much-needed discipline.
Sometimes we wrongly assume that discipline gets in the way of
showing our children love. But the reality is that a lack of discipline is
unkind and unloving.

"Before I was afflicted I went astray," scripture says, "but now I
keep Your Word." Affliction, apparently, is one thing that created a
change in this psalmist's behavior.

It's okay to "afflict" our children—with a loss of privileges or a few
extra chores—to teach them a lesson. Of course, our little darlings
may not like us at that moment. But ultimately we are showing more
genuine love than any amount of "friendship parenting" ever would.

*Heavenly Father, I lean on and rely on You
to help me parent my child. Grant me wisdom
to know when and what kind of discipline to use. Amen.*

Budget Breaker

Then said the LORD unto Moses, Behold, I will rain bread from heaven for you; and the people shall go out and gather a certain rate every day, that I may prove them, whether they will walk in my law, or no.

EXODUS 16:4 KJV

The month lasted longer than the paycheck. The grocery bill exceeded the budget. Childcare expenses surpassed the rent. It's not an easy road to travel, yet one that many of us walk.

Isn't it interesting that we can trust God for eternal life, yet find it harder to trust Him for help with the mortgage?

In the Old Testament, God told the wandering Israelites He would feed them "manna from heaven" but with one caveat: He would only allow them to gather enough food for one day. No storing food away for the dreaded "what if's" of tomorrow. They would simply have to trust their God to faithfully supply their needs.

They didn't always pass the "trust test"—and neither do we. But thankfully, God is faithful in spite of us! He will meet our needs when we come to Him in simple trust. Then we can bask in His faithfulness.

Father, Your Word promises to supply all my needs.
I trust You in spite of the challenges I see.
You are ever faithful. Thank You!

Do as I Do!

" 'These people honor me with their lips,
but their hearts are far from me.' "
MATTHEW 15:8 NLT

---

*B*ecause I'm the mom, that's why!"

We've all known mothers—perhaps we've been them ourselves—
who expect their children simply to obey orders, even when the
moms don't live up to their own standards. For example, we teach
our children not to lie. But what will they think when they overhear
us fibbing to get out of a commitment? The surest way for us to lose
respect and erode the very values we're trying to instill is to expect one
thing from our child while doing some other thing ourselves.

Children innately follow mom. And they often allow mom's behavior,
more than her words, to shape who they become. What might your
child's behavior say about your home? Is it filled with joy and respect,
or grumpiness and cursing? Are loyalty and honesty exemplified in daily
choices, or are "harmless" lies and excuses the norm?

As moms, we need to live our own lives above reproach before we
can expect godly behavior and good choices from each of our children.
May our words and actions always be ones that we would be proud to
see repeated by our child. . .because they will be!

Lord, please show me the ways in which I am not living
up to my own expectations. Help me be a good example
and a mom who deserves respect and obedience.

Casseroles and Kids

*"Physical training is good, but training for godliness is much better,
promising benefits in this life and in the life to come."*

1 Timothy 4:8 nlt

❋

The recipe is generations old, and it works perfectly: Grandma's creamy chicken casserole tastes exactly the same each time it's made. Whether Aunt Becky or Cousin Steve does the cooking, as long as they follow the recipe, the casserole turns out the same—delicious.

Raising children, however, is different. It's not simply a matter of following a "recipe." How many of us have seen a friend or family member carefully choose which television programs to watch, review school assignments for inappropriate material, scrutinize their children's friends, maybe even pursue private education or homeschooling, all in an effort to turn out perfect children? But there are times when at least one of those kids will go astray.

Why would such a child walk away? What makes the difference? Perhaps the "missing ingredient" is a freedom to choose.

We can meticulously follow a child-rearing "recipe" and still have a young person walk away from what he or she has been taught. What's most important for us as single moms is perseverance. We must never give up—forging ahead without unnecessary guilt over real or perceived mistakes.

Raising children is never as simple as following a recipe.

❋

*Father God, I surrender my children and my parenting
skills to You. Please enable me to do the best
I can and leave the rest in Your hands. Amen.*

Cabbage Patch Love

"I have loved you," says the LORD.
"But you ask, 'How have you loved us?'"
MALACHI 1:2 NIV

Mouth gaping open, Jamie stared at the array of Cabbage Patch dolls at the toy store. She examined each doll until she came to an infant boy, complete with birth certificate. "I want this one. His birthday is the same day as mine." Her mother bought the doll, and Jamie doted on it, "feeding" it with the tiny bottle and wiping its face clean. She carried the doll at all times and bragged about it to everyone she met.

Imagine if such a doll could speak. Would it say to Jamie, "You say you love me, but I don't feel loved. How do you love me?"

Sometimes we ask God the same question. "Of course we know You love us, but with everything that's happened, we don't always feel loved."

God has a ready answer: "Before I created Adam, I chose you, as I once chose Jacob instead of Esau. Not only did I choose you, I also adopted you into my family. I gave My Son to make you Mine. I am always with you."

When we examine the facts, it's obvious that God loves us. He longs for us to love Him back. Let's open our eyes—and hearts—to that perfect love.

Father, You chose us to be Your own. You love us with all the tender compassion of a doting Father. Let us rest in Your love.

Wise Guys

Have we read many headlines that include the words *wisdom* and *prudence*? Few "Ten Ways to Succeed" lists feature them—especially if we're talking about God's wisdom and prudence as defined in the Bible.

"Don't be so narrow-minded!" Coworkers laugh when we refuse to compromise Christian standards of honesty and diligence.

"The Bible? You've got to be kidding!" Friends roll their eyes. "It's about a zillion years old! What's the Bible got to do with today?" They pat us on the shoulder. "You need some fun in your life. Do what works for you."

God loves us, and He cares about our individual needs—and our fun! But His plan often stretches far beyond "what works" for each of us. If we choose to believe God and walk in His ways, He helps us deal with our weakness as we accept the scary challenges looming before us. God makes safe paths for our feet. But those who rebel against God stumble over His truth. The Word that heals us hurts unbelievers—and no one can offer them true relief until they "get wise" by turning back to God.

Father, even when I don't understand Your wisdom, help me believe Your loving heart. I pray for my friends who don't know You that they, too, may walk in safety.

Sleep on It

It is of the LORD's mercies that we are not consumed,
because his compassions fail not. They are new
every morning: great is thy faithfulness.

LAMENTATIONS 3:22–23 KJV

Sleep on it." Researchers have found that to be sound advice. They
believe that sleep helps people sort through facts, thoughts, and
memories, providing a clearer look at the big picture upon waking.
Sleep also separates reality from emotions like fear and worry, which
can cloud our thinking and interfere with rational decision-making.
Scientifically speaking, sleep is good medicine.

For Christians, the biological effects of sleep are outweighed
by the spiritual benefits of the new day God gives us. At the end of
an exhausting day, after the worries and the pressures of life have
piled high, we may lie down, feeling as though we can't take another
moment of stress. But God's Word tells us that His great mercy will
keep our worries and problems from consuming us.

Through the never-ending compassion of God, His faithfulness
is revealed afresh each morning. We can rise with renewed vigor. We
can eagerly anticipate the new day, leaving behind the concerns of
yesterday.

Heavenly Father, thank You for giving me a new measure of Your
mercy and compassion each day so that my concerns don't
consume me. I rest in You, and I lay my burdens at Your feet.

Nile Crocodiles

When she saw that he was a fine child, she hid him for three months. But when she could hide him no longer, she got a papyrus basket for him and coated it with tar and pitch. Then she placed the child in it and put it among the reeds along the bank of the Nile. His sister stood at a distance to see what would happen to him.

EXODUS 2:2–4 NIV

How did Moses' mother do it? How did she feel as she gently placed Moses into a (hopefully) waterproof basket and then lowered him into the murky waters of the Nile River?

Then how could she walk away? It was a dangerous river. All around swarmed birds, insects, and the frightening Nile crocodiles. How could his mother have resisted clutching that basket to her breast? Clearly, there was no other alternative for her.

Our children face risks, too, in their own rivers of life. The dangers are different than those Baby Moses may have encountered, but they're just as real: terrorists, car accidents, drugs and alcohol, even guns at school.

God had a plan for Moses' life. He wasn't like Miriam, watching her younger brother from far off; God had His hands on that little boy's basket the entire time. He has our children in His hands, too.

Thank You, Lord, that I can surrender my children to the dangers of life, knowing that You have a plan for them just as You did for Moses.

Real Love

I trust in God's unfailing love for ever and ever.
PSALM 52:8 NIV

We use the word *love* an awful lot. "I *love* your new purse," or "I *love* that dress on you," or "I *love* Hershey's Kisses." I bet if you kept track, you'd find yourself using the word *love* more than a dozen times each day. Because we use it so much, *love* has lost some of its punch, some of its luster, some of its meaning.

But real love—the God kind of love—is so much more than the "love" that has become so clichéd in our culture. The God kind of love is an everlasting love. His love stretches as far as the east is from the west. His love is deeper than the deepest ocean. His love is higher than the highest mountain. His love covers a multitude of sins. His love is unconditional. His love is truly awesome!

Now that's the kind of love I want to walk in. How about you? I want to receive the Father's love, and I want to extend His love to others—especially to my children. As moms, we should have the aroma of love. So if your love aroma is a little funky (like that green cheese in the back of the fridge), ask God to refresh your love today!

Lord, I pray that Your love—the real thing—shines in me and through me. Amen.

Serendipity

A happy heart makes the face cheerful.

PROVERBS 15:13 NIV

Can you remember the last time you laughed in wild abandon? Better yet, when was the last time you did something fun, outrageous, or out of the ordinary?

Women often become trapped in the cycle of routine, and soon we lose our spontaneity. Children, on the other hand, are innately spontaneous. Giggling, they splash barefoot in rain puddles. Wide-eyed, they watch a kite soar toward the treetops. They make silly faces without inhibition; they see animal shapes in rock formations. In essence, they possess the secret of serendipity.

A happy heart turns life's situations into opportunities for fun. For instance, if a storm snuffs out the electricity, light a candle and play games, tell stories, or just enjoy the quiet. When we seek innocent pleasures, we glean the benefits of a happy heart.

Jesus said, "I am come that they might have life, and that they might have it more abundantly" (John 10:10 KJV). God wants us to enjoy life, and when we do, it lightens our load and changes our countenance.

So try a bit of whimsy just for fun. And rediscover the secret of serendipity.

Dear Lord, because of You, I have a happy heart. Lead me to do something fun and spontaneous today! Amen.

Forgiveness Every Day

*Nevertheless my lovingkindness will I not utterly
take from him, nor suffer my faithfulness to fail.*
PSALM 89:33 KJV

Amy tried everything she could to get the little boy to learn to tie his shoes. She had sat with him for hours. There was nothing she could do to make him understand. Finally, she lost all patience and walked off, mad. His shoe-tying education would have to come from someone else with a lot more patience and endurance!

We may give up on each other, but it is comforting to know that God never gives up on us. His offer of forgiveness is open to us today and every day to come. Even though we reject the offer or do things that are frustrating and displeasing to Him, He never gives up. He asks us daily to follow Him until the day we finally do. Thank goodness His patience is without bounds.

*Though I push the patience of others to the limits, I am glad
to know that I have not pushed Yours, Lord. Continue to
forgive me, Lord. I am weak and foolish, and only
Your great love keeps me going. Amen.*

Waiting

Blessed are all who wait for him!
ISAIAH 30:18 NIV

*S*ome studies indicate we spend a total of *three years* of our lives just waiting!

That may seem hard to believe. But consider a typical day, with a few minutes stopped at traffic signals, a half hour in the doctor's waiting room, more time yet in a bottlenecked check-out line at the grocery store.

Some of us can handle that waiting through a natural patience. Others? Forget it.

Yet waiting is an inevitable part of everyone's life. And it's a necessary part, too. We wait nine months for a baby's birth. We wait for wounds to heal. We wait for our children to mature. And we wait for God to fulfill His promises.

Waiting for God to act is a familiar theme in scripture. Abraham and Sarah waited for a baby until a birth became humanly impossible. But it wasn't impossible to God. Joseph languished, unjustly accused, in Pharaoh's prison, while God ordained a far-reaching drought that would force Joseph's family to Egypt for survival. David spent years hiding from King Saul, but he matured into a wise and capable warrior during that time.

As frustrating as waiting can be, God is always at work on our behalf. Waiting time isn't wasted time. Whatever we might be waiting for—the salvation of our kids, provision for a physical need, a godly partner to help us with our parenting—we can wait with expectancy, trusting in God's timing.

By Your grace, Lord, help me to do the work You've called me to do and wait patiently for the good results You promise.

I've Fallen and I Can't Get Up

The godly may trip seven times, but they will get up again.
PROVERBS 24:16 NLT

❀

Years ago, a famous television commercial depicted an elderly woman who had fallen, but, try as she might, she just couldn't get back up. Thankfully, she wore a device that connected her to an outside source of help. All she had to do was push the button! The dear grandma was just one click away from rescue.

In our lives, too, there are times when we fall down—not physically, but emotionally, spiritually, and relationally. We fall in our attempts to parent; we fall in our struggle with particular temptations. We may fall as we try to climb the ladder of success or in our effort to lead a consistently godly life.

But in whatever area we wrestle, however many times we fall, our heavenly Father never gives up on us. He never leaves us to ourselves, to stagger to our feet alone. God is always present with us, encouraging us to keep trying—regardless of past failures—picking us up, dusting us off, and setting us on our way again.

He is better than any button we could ever push!

❀

Heavenly Father, it's such a comfort to know You will never leave me or forsake me. You are closer than the clothes I wear. I love You, Lord.

New Every Day

"See, I am doing a new thing!
Now it springs up; do you not perceive it?"
ISAIAH 43:19 NIV

One of the blessings of motherhood is watching our children grow. Changes come quickly in infancy—the first tooth, the first word, the first step. Later, we see the first friendship, the first day at school, the first line in a class play. Eventually our precious babies will become teenagers, head off to high school, and then leave home. Then we'll get to enjoy the process all over again, as grandmothers.

God wants us to approach all of life with the same fresh wonder. If every baby affirms that God wants the world to go on, and every rainbow is a reminder of God's promise, every dawn represents a new start.

In fact, God gives us countless opportunities to start over. The word *new* appears over 150 times in the Bible. He puts a new song in our mouths (Psalm 33:3). He gives us a new heart and makes us new creatures in Christ (2 Corinthians 5:17). At the end of time, He will create a new heaven and a new earth (Revelation 21:1).

Instead of worrying about the past, God wants us to long for what will be. He is the God of all things new.

Eternal God, every day is a new opportunity from You.
Teach me to rejoice in what You promise us.

Weather "Mom"

"When I smiled at them, they scarcely believed it;
the light of my face was precious to them."
JOB 29:24 NIV

A dark and gloomy sky in the morning may set the tone for an unproductive and disappointing day. But a bright sunny sky can add hope and promise to the day's outlook.

So it is in the home.

Mom's face is the forecast for the day—and the children's radar is always ready to take a reading. A gloomy mom indicates hopelessness and an expectation of failure, but a cheerful mom brings joy and eagerness to the day's outlook.

Attitude alone may not change our circumstances. But it can affect how we perceive things—and completely alter our final results. When we meet tough times with a cheerful, positive attitude, we can expect success and growth rather than failure and loss.

Perhaps we should examine our own habits. Do we mope around our homes with the "storm clouds" of long faces and gloomy dispositions? Or do we face each new day (and each new challenge) brightly with a sunshiny, eager confidence?

We set the forecast. May we reflect in our faces the kind of day that honors ourselves, our families, and our God.

Heavenly Father, please help me to control my mood so that I can cheerfully lead my family through the day. Let my face reveal the hope and expectation I have in Your promises. Amen.

Faith Eyes

*Now faith is confidence in what we hope
for and assurance about what we do not see.*
HEBREWS 11:1 NIV

Think for a moment of things we can't see but we know are there.

There's the wind, for one. Its effects are obvious, as golden grain sways to and fro or fall leaves blow into the sky. And there's gravity, which pulls our kids' cups—full of red Kool-Aid, usually—right to the floor.

It's the same with faith, as we simply believe in what we do not see. God *says* He is faithful, and so His faithfulness exists. He gives us the signs of His unseen presence, and its effects surround us.

We read how the Israelites walked to the sea and, at Moses' command, the sea parted. They could have been killed—by the pursuing Egyptians or by the sea itself—but God made a safe way of escape for them.

What signs surround you, showing your God is real? Perhaps someone blessed you with money to pay a bill or purchase school supplies. Maybe your "guardian angel" caught your attention and helped you avoid a serious accident. Or perhaps your child prayed to accept the Lord.

Those are all signs of the faithfulness of God. Look around with your "faith eyes" and see the signs surrounding you.

*God, I struggle to have faith. Show me where You have
been faithful so my faith can be strengthened. I know You
are faithful, but today I'm asking for a special sign that
You have not forgotten me. Thank You, Father.*

Fill 'er Up—with Joy

*We also pray that you will be strengthened with all
his glorious power so you will have all the endurance
and patience you need. May you be filled with joy.*

COLOSSIANS 1:11 NLT

We've all had days when we feel exhausted on every level, when we've drained our emotional gas tanks bone dry. As Paul prayed for the Christians of Colosse, we need a filling of God's strength so we can keep going—and rediscover *joy*.

But when can we find time to refill our tank in a life of constant work and worry? We don't have enough time for the rat race itself, let alone a pit stop. But if we don't refuel, we'll stall out—and be of no use to anyone.

That means we have to learn to make time for ourselves. We can explore things that give us a lift. Some things, like listening to a favorite playlist as we drift off to sleep, take no extra time. Others, like a bubble bath, may require minor adjustments to our schedule. Maybe we'll want to spend time in the garden or call a friend. There are any number of ways to recharge our spiritual batteries.

Every week—perhaps every day—we must set aside time to refill our tanks. The joy of the Lord will be our reward.

*Lord of joy, we confess that we are tempted to work until
we fall apart. We pray that You will show us the
things that will give us the strength to go on.*

Letting Go, Letting God

For this is what the LORD, the God of Israel, says: "The jar of flour will not be used up and the jug of oil will not run dry until the day the LORD sends rain on the land."

1 KINGS 17:14 NIV

Too many times, the only peaceful moments in the day are when the children are asleep. Mom's worries, however, are not so easily set aside.

Being a mother means worrying about the children's health, their success in school, and their wisdom in picking friends. Will they make the right choices?

In the Bible, the widow of Zarephath had an even sharper concern. She had only enough flour to make one more meal for herself and her son. After that, only starvation awaited. Yet Elijah asked the woman to make that flour into a biscuit for *him*—with God's promise that, if she did, her food would never run out. She chose to trust, to turn her life and the life of her son over to the Lord.

Turning *our* children over to God—truly trusting Him—is undoubtedly one of the hardest steps a mom can take. Yet God is ever faithful and never changing. The Lord who helped a desperate widow three thousand years ago remains by our side today.

Father God, help us remember Your steadfast love and support and that You care for our children intimately and eternally. Remind us that You will not let us fall.

Answered Prayer

Do what the LORD wants, and he
will give you your heart's desire.
PSALM 37:4 CEV

---

*S*ometimes our heartfelt prayers receive a "yes" from God.
Sometimes, it's a "no." At other times, we get back only a "not yet."

Have you heard anyone quote today's scripture, saying that God
will give us the desires of our hearts? Some believe the verse means
that a Christian can ask for anything—health, money, possessions, you
name it—and get exactly what she wants. But this passage actually
teaches something much deeper.

Note the first part of Psalm 37:4 (NIV): "Delight yourself in the
LORD." A woman who truly delights herself in the Lord will naturally
have the desires of her heart—because her heart desires only God and
His will. Our Father takes no pleasure in the things of this world—
things that will all wither and die. Neither should we.

So what pleases God? He loves it when we witness for Him, live
right, and raise our children in His Word. If those are things that we
also truly desire, won't He grant us the "desires of our heart" and let
us see people brought into the kingdom? Won't we have a life rich in
spiritual growth and children who honor His name?

Lord, please help me see where my desires are not in
line with Your will—so that the things that I pursue
are only and always according to Your own desires.

Quiet Reflection

Stand in silence in the
presence of the Sovereign LORD.
ZEPHANIAH 1:7 NLT

As parents, we teach our children to enter a room with their ears, not their mouths—to listen before speaking. Though we are not always successful, we try to instill in them this important lesson in conversation etiquette. Because someone else may already be talking, our kids must learn to stop and listen before speaking.

This truth applies to our devotional life with God, as well. How often do we race into our "quiet time" with a laundry list of needs? Do we inform God of all that is wrong—of all we'd like Him to do—then declare our "amen" and leave the room? If we aren't careful, "quiet time" can become not an opportunity to linger in God's presence, but a whirlwind of quickly stated prayers.

When walking into our special time with God, let's make it a habit to relax for a bit. Listen for His voice, read a few verses from the Bible, and simply rest in His presence. It need not be a lengthy process— time is often in short supply for busy moms. But it is a matter of listening before speaking—a lesson in good manners that we, as well as our children, need to learn.

Holy Father, teach me to enter my time alone with You,
listening rather than speaking. Enable me to pour
out my heart to You, then rest in Your care.

My Steps

"His eyes are on the ways of mortals; he sees their every step."
JOB 34:21 NIV

❀

Tammy watched her son intently. She had been working with him over the past month, teaching him not to walk into the street without her. It had been a daunting lesson, but Tammy felt it was extremely valuable.

Today, the inevitable presented itself to Josh. He stood on the sidewalk, arms stretched toward the ball, his favorite, that had rolled into the street. Not for a second did Tammy's eyes wander from her son, watching for any quick movement toward the dangerous street. She held her breath and moved within arm's reach, lest he step out to retrieve his toy.

In the same way, our Father watches His children intently. Life sometimes feels as though *we* are wandering on a busy street with dangerous traffic zipping all around. But all the while, God keeps His eyes on us. He intently watches our every step, lest we fall. And when we do stumble, He is always within arm's reach—ready to catch us, love us, and teach us once again His perfect ways.

❀

Father, I may not know what direction my life will take or where my path may lead. I do know, though, that You never take Your eyes off me; You see every step I take, guiding me and directing me and catching me when I stumble. Thank You for loving me enough to keep Your eyes on me in this journey.

A Mom's Uniform

*Therefore we do not lose heart. Though outwardly we
are wasting away, yet inwardly we are being renewed day
by day. For our light and momentary troubles are achieving
for us an eternal glory that far outweighs them all.*

2 Corinthians 4:16–17 niv

When a young mother looks into her closet, she may notice that
the contents have miraculously rotated. The jeans, sweats, and comfy
shirts are now easily reachable in the front, while the untouched
business clothes and once-coveted white pants have somehow been
relegated to the memorabilia section in back. The dusty trophy of days
gone by—those white pants—will most likely not see the light of day
for many years, as peanut butter, crayon, and grape juice are now part
of the daily repertoire.

Does she retain the same value in the eyes of the world while
wearing the "uniform" of a mom? Perhaps not. But what is her worth
in the sight of the Lord? Moms need not measure their self-worth on
the scale that the world imposes: wealth, wardrobe, and worldly goods.
Rather, the true scale used to determine success is measured with
eternal glory. While outward appearances may seem to diminish when
business attire is traded for play clothes, inward appearances become
increasingly glorious as daily sacrifices are made in answer to the call
to motherhood.

*Lord, thank You for the privilege of being a mom. Help me to
remember that You value this role as one of Your highest callings and
greatest challenges. And help me to see myself as You see me. Amen.*